Things My ESOP Advisor
Never Told Me

What Your ESOP Advisors May Not Have Told You (But Should Have)

Things My ESOP Advisor
Never Told Me

What Your ESOP Advisors May Not Have Told You (But Should Have)

Patrick DeCraene
Joe Demetrius
Nancy Dittmer
Aziz El-Tahch
Kevin Long
Corey Rosen
James Staruck

The National Center for Employee Ownership
Oakland, California

This publication is designed to provide accurate and authoritative information in regard to the subject matter covered. It is sold with the understanding that the publisher is not engaged in rendering legal, accounting, or other professional service. If legal advice or other expert assistance is required, the services of a competent professional person should be sought.

Legal, accounting, and other rules affecting business often change. Before making decisions based on the information you find here or in any publication from any publisher, you should ascertain what changes might have occurred and what changes might be forthcoming. The NCEO's Web site (including the members-only area) and newsletter for members provide regular updates on these changes. If you have any questions or concerns about a particular issue, check with your professional advisor or, if you are an NCEO member, call or email us.

Things My ESOP Advisor Never Told Me
Patrick DeCraene, Joe Demetrius, Nancy Dittmer, Aziz El-Tahch, Kevin Long, Corey Rosen, and James Staruck

Book design by Scott Rodrick

Copyright © 2013 by The National Center for Employee Ownership. All rights reserved. Printed in the United States of America. No part of this book may be reproduced or transmitted in any form or by any means, electronic or mechanical, including photocopying, recording, or by any information storage and retrieval system, without prior written permission from the publisher.

The National Center for Employee Ownership
1736 Franklin Street, 8th Floor
Oakland, CA 94612
(510) 208-1300
(510) 272-9510 (fax)
Web site: www.nceo.org

ISBN: 978-1-938220-09-8

Contents

Introduction   1
Corey Rosen

1. How Many Lawyers Does It Take To...?   3
   Kevin Long

2. Best Practices and Common Mistakes in ESOP Company Valuations   17
   Aziz El-Tahch and Joe Demetrius

3. What You Should Expect from Your ESOP TPA   31
   Nancy Dittmer

4. Best Practices for ESOP Trustees   45
   James Staruck and Patrick DeCraene

   About the Authors   59

   About the NCEO   63

Introduction

Corey Rosen

In late 2012, I met with an ESOP company's inside fiduciaries. Their concerns had focused on distribution rules, but in the course of our conversation, I found that:

- Their appraisal report was all of 15 pages long, and only one of the three trustees had actually read it. Their ESOP attorney apparently must have assumed that they were following standard procedures about valuation, which requires trustees to read, understand, and question the report as needed. A standard appraisal report is 70 or more pages long, with detailed discussions about methodologies and data in which all conclusions are based on well-elaborated arguments, not simply conclusory statements.

- Their company was an S corporation, and the ESOP owned 95% of the shares. The 5% owner did not want to sell because his corporate attorney had told him he should hold on to some shares for control reasons. The company had been only breaking even because it was repaying the ESOP note, but now it would start making profits. If it made distributions to the 5% owner to pay taxes, the ESOP would have to get 19 times as much. Moreover, the control issue is bogus—the 5% share had no practical impact on control.

- One of the reasons the company was only breaking even was that it was paying off its ESOP loan very quickly. No one had told the company that the loan could have been arranged so that there was one loan to the company and another loan to the ESOP with a longer term that would spread out how quickly employees accumulated shares. By not doing this, they were creating a major have/have not problem in which employees who were in the ESOP in the early stages would accumulate much larger ESOP account balances than later hires because by then most or all the shares would have been paid for and released.

ESOPs can be complex plans with lots of moving parts. It is easy to overlook something you should or could do because your advisors, who may be very well qualified, forget to tell you or assume that you would know this because another advisor would have told you. Moreover, many ESOP companies have one or more advisors who have limited ESOP experience and thus may well miss an important obligation or opportunity.

This book is designed to help you know exactly what your advisors might not be telling you and what they should be. Each chapter starts with a story about a company's ESOP gone wrong and what could have been done. It then follows with step-by-step descriptions of what you need to expect from each of your key advisors—lawyers, administrators, appraisers, and trustees.

Chapter 1

How Many Lawyers Does It Take To…?

Kevin Long

LeBlanc Lighting was a successful commercial lighting operation that had set up an ESOP in the 1980s, not too many years after ESOPs were given a statutory basis in the Employee Retirement Income Security Act of 1974 (ERISA).[1] It had been partly employee-owned for a couple of decades as a C corporation. Its plan and its stock transactions had occurred over a series of years under the advice of an ESOP consulting firm and an ERISA attorney who periodically provided documents to sell small minority interests in the company to the ESOP. Nothing fancy, no leveraged tax-deferred rollover transactions. The ESOP seemed to work well. Benefits were paid, and compliance was handled by consultants. The appraiser for many years, referred in by the consultants long ago, was a sole practitioner. The trustee committee was comprised of managers and often included two of the non-ESOP owners. With the advent of S corporation ESOPs in 1998, and the aging of the shareholders, it was time to have the ESOP buy the rest of the stock, so the employees could finally own the rest of the company.

True to form, the ESOP appraiser valued the stock and the ESOP bought the rest of the shares, with the ESOP borrowing some money from the company and the sellers taking notes for the rest. The trustee committee had the same members for several years, namely the CFO, the HR manager, and the president, who was one of the remaining selling shareholders. Everything seemed routine, except that the sale was larger,

---

1. This company is fictional, but the fact pattern is based on real-life situations encountered by ESOP companies.

the notes were bigger, and the company was going to become tax-free. The company guaranteed the seller notes. Because of this, the appraiser opined at the transaction that the value for a tax-free company was higher and a control premium was warranted.

As sometimes happens, the company's prospects dimmed and cash flow got tight. The company lost some major accounts, and the stock value dropped. The company needed working capital; it looked for lenders and asked the seller's family to restructure debt. But banks wouldn't lend without the sellers taking some concessions. The stock value was challenged by employees and the U.S. Department of Labor. It was alleged that the S corporation tax attributes were not properly accounted for in the appraisal, and that the drop in business was not prudently forecast. The control premium was challenged as too high because the ESOP did not get actual control. As it turned out, not all the named trustees voted to approve the transaction. The HR manager wasn't aware she had been named to the ESOP trustee committee. There was no insurance in place for the board and the trustees. After all, it had been a peaceful ESOP company for so many years. Decisions had always been made by consensus.

Restructuring, refinancing, investigation, and litigation defense continued. Ultimately, the company was sold to resolve the multiple conflicts.

The Role of the Attorney in the ESOP World

The roles of attorneys in the ESOP world are driven by balancing the myriad choices of transactions and succession planning strategies with the applicable federal and state laws. Like any business succession plan, an ESOP has a complexity that requires knowledgeable counsel. But the ESOP's particular complexity is a tradeoff for the immense benefits and advantages that it offers to companies, their employees, and their shareholders who ultimately are able to buy and sell stock and pay benefits in a tax-advantaged fashion.

An ESOP involves two federal statutes, the Internal Revenue Code (the "Code") and ERISA. ERISA provides requirements for all retirement plans, of which the ESOP is considered one. That is one set of legal issues, but ESOPs also often serve as succession plans and/or employee incentive plans. ESOP companies also have to deal with state corporate law and the various business and contract laws that arise in any business and financing transaction. Finally, the fact that the ESOP is administered by fiduciaries whose duties are scrutinized under the highest standards of the law by both the federal regulators and in civil suits fuels the need to ensure that all legal issues are properly, prudently, and timely addressed.

But with this particular complexity and the multiple parties involved in an ESOP company structure or transaction, how many lawyers does an ESOP require, who do they work for, and which one does what? Can one lawyer represent multiple parties? Can an ESOP be set up simply enough that we don't need multiple lawyers? What about conflicts of interest and the attorney/client privilege?

The best way to answer these questions and understand the use of ESOP lawyers is to look at each constituency's needs over the life cycle of an ESOP or in the context of different transactions. The parties, at a minimum, that need legal advice in all ESOP contexts are:

- The company sponsoring the ESOP
- The ESOP fiduciaries: the trustee and the administrator
- Selling shareholders
- Other shareholders

Company Sponsoring the ESOP

Forming the ESOP

The decision to adopt an ESOP is a company "plan sponsor" decision, a business decision under general business and corporate law. The board will decide to initiate an ESOP to serve various purposes. Often this issue of ESOP or no ESOP starts with the advice of a non-lawyer consultant but results in an attorney drafting the ESOP plan and trust documents. In other cases, the attorney will be the primary advisor to the company on the merits of an ESOP. Much of the consulting advice that is given in this context is actually legal advice, so it's important to be sure that you are not being underadvised.

If any advice is based on the Code or ERISA, it is best to ask your attorneys whether they agree with the consulting advice you are being given. Again, this relates to the fact that the ESOP is a retirement plan and a new shareholder.

The primary ERISA legal issue that corporate counsel has to advise on is the appointment and monitoring of ESOP fiduciaries, which is a board of directors responsibility and fiduciary duty. So, if corporate counsel is not by nature an ERISA attorney, or an ESOP attorney, he or she should be mindful that the overall performance of the plan and transaction can come back to haunt the corporate client's board of directors.

Clients may have recourse against their lawyers for inadequate or bad advice, and lesser recourse against non-lawyer consultants. Lawyers in all jurisdictions must carry malpractice insurance. Non-attorney consultants are not required to. However, it may be too expensive to expect your attorneys to advise on the quantitative aspects of their advice. Calculations of tax benefits and cash flow assumptions should in most cases be performed by financial or tax advisors, as long as they are applying the Code provisions correctly.

In LeBlanc's case, forming the ESOP was likely very straightforward— way back when. But major changes in direction or in tax laws require rethinking. Particularly in a change-of-control setting, corporate governance matters must be addressed so that valuation issues like a control premium are in the right setting. The board also has the fiduciary duty to oversee trustees. Counsel should have advised the board of this ERISA duty and removed or required the resignation of any selling shareholder from the trustee committee. Could this advice come from the long-term ESOP lawyer relationship? Yes, without doubt. In fact, it is the kind of advice that either specialized ESOP counsel or just competent corporate counsel would or should spot. There should also never be a ball dropped in appointing fiduciaries, with all of the fiduciaries knowing and being advised that they are appointed and engaged and involved and responsible. No one should wake up the morning after and learn that he or she was a fiduciary in an ESOP transaction.

Corporate and Contract Issues

Beyond the drafting of the plan document, installing an ESOP ultimately must result in corporate counsel advising the board of directors on the impact on the company of creating another shareholder. The ESOP as a new shareholder may trigger any one of a range of issues under state corporate law and contract law. Listing them all is beyond the scope of this chapter, but some of most simple examples include revising the articles, bylaws, shareholder agreements, and employment contracts with management. Adding a new shareholder can affect the rights of existing shareholders by way of dilution or interference with existing capital structures. It is possible that the attorneys handling the ESOP planning in general will perform these tasks and offer this advice to accommodate a new ESOP and ESOP transactions. In many cases, existing corporate counsel will be called upon to provide this support based upon their invaluable historical relationships with the board of directors and knowledge of the company's operations. In more complex corporate structures, corporate counsel may need to restructure or create new entities so that the ESOP can be sponsored by the right corporation to cover the right employees. Finally, there may be regulatory concerns in a company's industry that must be addressed before an ESOP is installed.

The change-in-control transaction for LeBlanc was a fork in its road. At this point, it became critical to determine whether the company needed separate counsel from the ESOP or whether the ESOP, as buyer, could have its counsel take on the corporate work to restructure matters to suit the ESOP after the transaction. The degree of involvement and control of the former shareholders should have been defined. If the ESOP lawyer was providing historical advice to the company but the selling shareholders felt close to their advice, fresh counsel might be necessary. Sometimes the lawyer's relationship may correctly be with the right party, but it may still become uncomfortable in a transaction setting. The sellers at this point might also need their own counsel to advise them on their employment agreements or voting rights or role in governance going forward.

Transaction Issues

Obviously, the corporation is an integral part of any ESOP transaction and will have primarily commercial law concerns, but there will be ERISA considerations as well. Transaction lawyers (ESOP or not) can have varying roles depending on the sophistication and size of the company. For example they may handle legal negotiations with the bankers if the transaction is large enough or even go so far as to assist in finding the best loan for a transaction, though primarily based on the legal terms of the financing, not the commercial availability. Some ESOP lawyers will work on financing solicitations for their clients, but that is not typical for ESOP lawyers.

When positioning a company in an ESOP transaction, counsel must look ahead for issues that may arise in future scenarios, such as refinancing, amending ESOPs, mergers and acquisitions, and work-outs with creditors and sellers. Under many state laws regulating lawyers (law practice is regulated state by state), a lawyer cannot represent both the corporation and a majority shareholder unless the corporation waives the conflict of interest. Conflicts are discussed later in this chapter.

LeBlanc had a fairly easy transaction structure. However, it may have been underadvised in a number of areas. Even though it did not seek bank financing for the transaction, the ESOP raises corporate finance issues for the future. Counsel for the corporation must ensure that all of the surrounding agreements, such as guarantees of ESOP notes, leave room for the company's future needs; for example, subordination agreements with enough leeway to allow the company to obtain working capital and not be forced to sell. Or perhaps counsel should advise in the transaction to not use company cash, but use bank debt, so the company has "dry powder" for future needs. Is this a legal issue? Could this be handled by ESOP counsel? Perhaps. In this context, it would clearly be difficult for corporate counsel to be the seller's counsel as well. In some cases sellers recognize they need to accommodate the golden goose in order to get paid. But the mechanisms need to be put in place so that the unforeseen scenarios (which always happen) can be negotiated.

ESOP Fiduciaries

It almost goes without saying that ESOP fiduciaries, including the trustee and the administrator, need specialized representation. The ERISA and income tax issues are highly regulated. The most fundamental areas of advice deal with complying with the Code and ERISA on the fair market value determinations and the overall prudence of the transaction. Lawyers won't tell you what is prudent, but they will advise you as you go through the process to make the prudent decision.

The S corporation rules affect how appraisers value ESOP shares, and in LeBlanc's case, arguably both the ESOP lawyer and the consultants should have helped the trustees ensure that the change in appraisal premises affected their duty and their decisions. Legal advice in appraisal due diligence should have uncovered the issues. Particularly in a change of control, counsel should advise on tax and financial deal points, which become legal issues. One of the leading ESOP valuation cases stands for the proposition that the trustees are responsible for the assumptions, methods, and calculations of the fair market value of the ESOP stock. ESOP counsel should have guided the LeBlanc committee through the valuation process carefully. This was not a business-as-usual transaction. Lawyers are not appraisers, but they can and should support the appraisal process. A key point here is that the seller was a trustee for some time, and this transaction represented a change-in-control premium. One might argue that retaining a new appraiser was the best practice to follow. Perhaps counsel should have urged LeBlanc to engage an independent trustee, even at the risk of the new trustee engaging its own new counsel.

Counsel for the fiduciaries must also advise on the range of issues, from transaction contracts to the commercial aspects of an ESOP transaction, that are not themselves ERISA matters. They may be matters of the terms of financing documents and terms of employment agreements that, after the deal closes, will be in place at the company the ESOP is buying. The ESOP's attorney's role may be as much a corporate counsel role, representing a shareholder, as it is a role advising an ERISA fiduciary.

Similarly, during the transaction process, the ESOP attorney's critical role is to support the trustee in the due diligence process. Counsel must handle the legal due diligence, and the trustee must handle the factual due diligence. This may require expertise in areas such as environmental or patent law. ESOP counsel must either handle this or feel comfortable that corporate counsel can properly deliver due diligence disclosure on behalf of the ESOP so as not to duplicate legal efforts. Ultimately, the client, not counsel, must discover facts underlying the transaction, but counsel must help guide and advise the trustees as they do their legwork.

Selling Shareholders

It almost goes without saying that selling shareholders require representation on the flip side of all of the ESOP's transaction issues. The commercial law issues include the terms of the transaction, loan agreements, collateral, and guaranty agreements. The entire ESOP planning process will trigger a need for estate planning and tax advice that is personal to the sellers, and not at all relevant to the ESOP. ESOPs are often relevant in complex estate planning structures and may be recommended or implemented by attorneys with specialized practices that include estate planning. It is very common for the seller's counsel to be the lawyer or firm that handles these personal legal matters for the sellers. Handling the seller-side issues in a stock sale transaction is typically within the area of competence for such lawyers or their firms.

Unfortunately, all too often sellers who are embedded in the company feel that the ESOP lawyers working with their consultants should be able to get the work done as corporate ESOP counsel, or as ESOP counsel, and the sellers will be fine and won't need their own lawyers. The best practice is that sellers clearly and always have their own counsel. It is the first and best additional lawyer to bring to the table. It starts to free up the other advisors to do their job with minimized conflicts (real or perceived).

In LeBlanc's case, perhaps the lack of separate personal counsel during the transaction ultimately worked to the sellers' benefit. Perhaps a forced sale of the company allowed them the liquidity event they would have chosen if they had their druthers. In any event, an impasse with the sellers played out to end the ESOP.

After the Dust Settles

Long after an ESOP is in place, most of the parties will need occasional legal advice on matters affected by the ESOP. Most frequently it is the ESOP and the corporation that need advice. Which lawyers should remain responsible, and how proactively? In many if not most cases, the ongoing maintenance of an ESOP is fronted by a third-party administrator and an appraiser (if not an independent trustee) that will from time to time come across needs that exceed their scope and will refer out issues to counsel. Companies would be wise to heed such referrals and be sure they have counsel standing by. In addition, ESOP documents need regular service, since every five years they are resubmitted to the Internal Revenue Service for approval of their tax-qualified status.

Finally, there is no substitute for having counsel regularly keeping in touch as the law changes or planning opportunities arise. Not all lawyers are proactive planners, but in this specialized area, very often they are. It is a safe presumption, though not guaranteed, that the attorneys who have been instrumental in crafting the ESOP plan will stay on board to notify the client of changes in the law that affect them.

Conflicts of Interest

Everyone has opinions about lawyers, but almost universally, when it is clear that someone truly needs one, he or she wants the best. Unfortunately it is difficult to predict when or why you may need one in the future, or how you may come to need one if the ESOP legal work isn't adequate up front. But which parties involved with an ESOP need their own attorney, and when can you share the services of an attorney? As with many legal questions, it depends.

Rules of professional responsibility for lawyers (which are state-based but for the most part uniform across the U.S.) permit a lawyer to represent multiple parties facing "potential conflicts of interest," and in some cases "actual" conflicts of interest, if adequate disclosure and waivers are obtained. The question is when you should not waive a potential conflict with another party. Some conflicts should never be waived, in my opinion. An ESOP, as buyer, should never share counsel with the seller. Unlike non-ESOP transactions in which (surprisingly) this sometimes happens, there is an ERISA and tax reason for not doing so, i.e., the prudence rules and prohibited transaction rules, which are closely examined and can be painfully enforced.

But what about the other relationships? And how clearly are these conflicts identified, disclosed, and waived in an ESOP transaction? Given the wide array of areas of legal issues, it may be possible for ERISA counsel to provide advice to the corporation and also to some of the ESOP fiduciaries on certain matters such as plan design, but perhaps not on ESOP transaction structure or in the context of negotiations. For example, if special classes of stock are being created for the ESOP transaction, the ESOP trustees may want to negotiate certain terms of those securities with separate representation, because they are inherently buyer-versus-seller concerns, even though they may be designed by corporate counsel in conjunction with the financial advisors.

And what of the common situation in which company counsel has been personal counsel to a shareholder before the advent of the ESOP? All client constituencies should ask, "Who do you represent, and can I rely on your advice? And is our advice privileged?" There is no easy answer, but the best rule is to assume the seller's counsel is always the seller's counsel. It may be necessary to get "fresh counsel" for either the company or management when putting the ESOP transaction together. Privilege itself is discussed below.

One important litmus test to use when assessing the need for separate or multiple counsel is to ask: If this transaction is examined or challenged (whether for a good or bad reason), will it be clear that each party was adequately advised? Will any of the parties' judgment appear compromised?

Attorney/Client Privilege

Privilege is often misunderstood and is subject to special rules in the ESOP context. Fundamentally, a client is entitled to have advice of counsel protected by privilege, unless the client waives it. Consenting to dual representation can compromise that privilege. If there are concerns about wanting to keep advice protected, then counsel should not be shared.

More significantly, attorney/client advice is not privileged if it is advice from counsel to the fiduciary of a plan, like an ESOP. The theory is that the privilege ultimately runs in favor of the participants and beneficiaries of the trust, not the trustee. If a trustee feels a need for personal advice that is protected and confidential, then he or she should have personal counsel. This almost always happens if a trustee is sued—he or she retains personal defense counsel. In the context of a transaction, however, this is not typical. The advice to the trustee is for the purpose of the trustee prudently serving the ESOP. Ultimately, that advice will be available for review if the transaction is examined later, which is good. A trustee will want to be able to show he or she obtained proper advice and acted prudently. Therefore, the best guideline to follow is that if ERISA legal advice is being obtained, assume that at some point it will not be protected by privilege if it can be established that the client is acting as a fiduciary to the plan.

Other parties, like the corporation, may obtain ESOP advice, and it may be protected by privilege. The corporation will need advice on the plan's formation or amendment and the planning options. That will be privileged because it is not fiduciary advice. However, ERISA advice the company receives in reviewing the performance of the trustee or the administrator may be advice in the administration of the plan, or "fiduciary advice" and may not be privileged. It is sometimes advisable to have counsel maintain separate corporate and ERISA files and matters for its clients.

So, how many lawyers did they need at LeBlanc? They were at least one short, potentially two. The sellers needed counsel. If they brought in an independent trustee, they would have had an ESOP attorney for just the ESOP. If they simply reconstituted the trustee committee, they would have had to decide whether they wanted new counsel or felt comfortable simply with the sellers having separate representation. As for the corporation, separate counsel there would depend on whether the ESOP counsel could assume that role as well, with the seller not opposing that conflict. The seller might insist that corporate counsel be neutral to the ESOP and the sellers. You may not always know ahead of time, but you will know if the lights go out.

(Appendix begins on next page)

Appendix

Legal Needs of the Parties

ESOP Fiduciary Needs	Seller Needs	Company Needs
General fiduciary duties		Same—must oversee fiduciaries
Appraisal/due diligence		Same—must oversee fiduciaries
Adequate consideration determination	Same—to avoid a prohibited transaction	Same—must oversee fiduciaries
Transaction prudence	Only for credit risk	Same—must oversee fiduciaries
Corporate governance	Risk of post-transaction control	Same—but duty to all shareholders, not just the ESOP
Transaction documents	Same—opposing	Same—as they affect company
Financing documents	Same—opposing	Same—may be primary party
Plan administration issues		Same—if the plan administrator
Participant communications		Same—if the plan administrator

Sample ESOP Transaction Documents You Will Need from Your Attorney

Please note: *The following lists are merely examples. In your own situation, additional documents may be needed, and not all of the documents below may apply. For example, several items assume that a seller is making the Section 1042 election.*

Background Documents

- Engagement letter between ERISA counsel and company and/or ESOP
- Conflict-of-interest disclosure letters and waiver
- Engagement agreement between professional trustee and company
- Engagement letter between trustee and appraiser

- Articles of incorporation (amended)
- Bylaws (amended)
- Voting trusts
- Directors and officers (D&O) insurance policy
- ERISA fiduciary insurance policy or rider to D&O

ESOP Transaction Documents

- Letter of intent
- Resolutions of the board of directors
- Trustee resolutions
- Shareholder resolutions
- ESOP plan document and summary plan description (SPD)
- Acceptance of administrative committee members
- Resignations of directors
- Stock purchase agreement
- Stock certificates
- Secured nonrecourse promissory note (ESOP loan)
- Secured nonrecourse promissory note (seller subordinate loan)
- Stock pledge and security agreement (ESOP loan)
- Stock pledge and security agreement (subordinate loan)
- Corporate guaranty
- Conditional assignment of pledge agreement and security agreement
- Indemnification agreement
- Employment agreement between company and CEO
- Phantom stock plan/deferred compensation agreement(s)
- Appraiser's transaction opinion letter (adequate consideration and fairness)

- Phantom stock plan grant agreements
- Corporate consent to election under Code Section 1042(b)(3)
- Statement of election under Code Section 1042
- Notarized statements of purchase under Section 1042

Bank Loan Documents

- Loan agreement
- Term promissory note
- Corporate continuing guaranty
- Security agreement for corporate assets
- Corporate authorization to obtain credit, grant security, guarantee or subordinate
- Subordination agreement (seller)
- Bank's revolving promissory note
- Account control agreement for 1042 collateral
- Security agreement (for 1042 reinvestment securities)

Chapter 2

Best Practices and Common Mistakes in ESOP Company Valuations

Aziz El-Tahch and Joe Demetrius

Recently, a friend of ours who serves as an ESOP trustee called to ask a favor. A valuation firm with whom she works had just delivered the valuation update report for ESOP administration purposes, and the conclusion of value was much higher than expected. It was so high that the trustee and the company's CEO were both concerned that the company wouldn't be able to satisfy its repurchase obligation while also making certain necessary capital investments without incurring a significant amount of debt. "Something doesn't seem quite right," she said. "Could you take a quick look at the analysis and let me know what you think?"

As it turns out, the valuation professional who performed the analysis works for a regional CPA firm without much specific experience in valuing ESOP-owned companies. In his analysis, he relied upon a single valuation method: the discounted cash flow (DCF) method. In his DCF method analysis, the valuation professional didn't tax-affect the subject company's projected cash flows under the premise that the company is a 100% ESOP-owned S corporation, and is thus exempt from federal income taxes—which is inconsistent with the standard of "fair market value" by which ESOP company valuations are bound. Worse, to calculate projected free cash flow, the valuation professional neglected to deduct the company's projected capital expenditures. It was therefore no surprise that the trustee and the CEO were concerned about the company's ability to make these investments, since these investments weren't reflected anywhere in the analysis. Since the valuation professional came to his conclusion by only using one valuation method, there were no other indications of value from alternative valuation methods to serve as a reasonableness check.

As we were discussing all of these various methodological and analytical flaws with our friend, she asked (with more than a hint of frustration), "how was I supposed to know all of this? After all, I'm not a valuation professional, and I want to be able to rely on my experts." The objective of this chapter is to provide a roadmap for people like our friend—employees of ESOP companies serving as "internal" ESOP trustees, third-party trustees with a limited valuation background, and corporate officers who need to understand the valuation to manage their business—as they review the annual valuation. To that end, this chapter (1) summarizes best practices that should be followed by the valuation firm and trustee in documenting the valuation process; (2) provides a list of questions that trustees should ask the valuation professional as they review the valuation report, plus specific areas within the analysis where the trustee should challenge the valuation professional; and (3) outlines some of the most common mistakes in valuation analyses performed for ESOP purposes.

Purpose of the ESOP Company Valuation and Documentation Requirements

ESOP company valuations are performed for a variety of purposes, including determining that the ESOP is not paying more than "adequate consideration" (i.e., fair market value) as part of an ESOP purchase, determining that the ESOP is not receiving less than adequate consideration as part of a company sale, and determining fair market value in connection with ongoing ESOP administration. Regardless of the purpose, the independent valuation firm hired by the ESOP trustee should have significant experience performing business valuations specifically for ESOP companies, and it should be actively involved in relevant ESOP industry organizations (such as the NCEO and the ESOP

Association) since these organizations provide the primary venues for ESOP company valuation experts to share best practices and stay up-to-date on recent developments in the field.

The work product provided by the valuation professional should conform to the U.S. Department of Labor's report content requirements and should therefore include:

- A summary of the valuation professional's qualifications;
- A description of the security being valued;
- The effective date of the valuation;
- The purpose of the valuation;
- A list of documents relied upon (and which should be retained by the valuation firm);
- A summary of valuation methods considered and relied upon;
- The specific factors considered by the valuation professional in performing the analysis; and
- The significance and relative weight of differing valuation methods.

The valuation firm and trustee should retain in their files any notes and materials from the management due diligence meetings as well as meeting minutes from the formal presentation to the trustee, whether or not the notes and materials make it into the valuation report.

Asking the Right Questions

In my introductory story, my friend wasn't able to detect the flaws in the valuation professional's analysis because, as she put it, "I'm not a valuation professional, and I want to be able to rely on my experts." And while this stance holds some practical appeal—after all, if the trustee *were* a valuation expert, he or she wouldn't need to hire a valuation firm—the trustee nevertheless has a duty to understand and remain engaged in the valuation process. Generally, ESOP fiduciaries cannot justify their reliance on the views of an independent financial advisor unless the fiduciary has read and understood the valuation report;

identified, questioned, and tested the underlying financial data and assumptions; verified that the conclusions are consistent with the data and analyses; and verified that the valuation report is internally consistent and makes sense.

The trustee can begin to fulfill his or her duty by asking the right questions. In every valuation analysis, there are many common areas where controversies can arise. The trustee can get a sense as to whether the valuation professional has adequately supported his or her assumptions in these areas by asking the right questions, some of which are outlined below:

Adjustments to Company Earnings

Questions to ask the valuation professional include:

- Why do you consider the adjustment nonrecurring or non-operating in nature?
- Is this adjustment consistent with valuations your firm prepares for other companies and for the subject company historically?
- Is this adjustment consistent with any adjustments made to the earnings of the guideline companies?

Some examples of common and supportable adjustments include:

- One-time litigation or settlement expense;
- Goodwill impairment;
- Unusual gain or loss on an asset sale; and
- Nonrecurring expenses related to a major transaction.

Selection and Weighting of Valuation Approaches

Questions to ask the valuation professional include:

- Of the three standard valuation approaches—the asset-based approach, the income approach, and the market approach—which ones did you rely upon, and why?

- Have there been any changes in the selected approaches since the previous valuation? If so, why?
- In your valuation conclusion, what relative weighting did you assign to each valuation approach and method, and why?

Some examples of common and supportable responses include:

- We did not rely on the asset-based approach because the subject company, as a going concern entity, has a high level of intangible value that would not be captured by this approach, such as established customer relationships, a trained and assembled workforce, and a well-known brand name.
- We assigned less weight to the market approach given the uniqueness of the subject company's business operations.
- We assigned less weight to the income approach because the company does not prepare detailed projections and has very limited visibility into future performance.

Market Approach Analyses

Questions to ask the valuation professional include:

- Why did you choose a particular financial metric—such as EBIT (earnings before interest and taxes), EBITDA (earnings before interest, taxes, depreciation, and amortization), or revenue—to apply multiples to? Why do you exclude certain other financial metrics?
- Why did you choose a particular time period—such as the most recent fiscal year, a five-year average, or the projected fiscal year—to analyze?
- Are the financial metrics and time periods you analyzed consistent with the prior valuation? And if not, why did you decide to make a change?
- Of the two generally accepted market approach methods—the guideline public company method and the guideline transaction method—which did you use, and why?

- How does the subject company compare to the guideline public companies and the guideline acquired companies in terms of risk, growth, and profitability, and how does this affect your selected multiples?
- How have the selected multiples changed since last year's analysis, and why?

Some examples of common and supportable responses include:

- The subject company is a financial services company with a substantial balance sheet, so a multiple of tangible book value (rather than an earnings- or cash flow-based multiple) was appropriate.
- The subject company is a service company with a very low level of capital expenditures and corresponding depreciation expenses, so a multiple of EBIT (as opposed to EBITDA) was appropriate.
- The company operates in a highly cyclical industry, so it was most appropriate to analyze five-year average financial results.
- The company operates in a growth industry and is gaining market share within that industry, so it was most appropriate to analyze the projected fiscal year financial results.
- We could not identify a meaningful number of guideline transactions with financial disclosure to perform a supportable guideline transaction method analysis, and those transactions we did identify were acquired by strategic buyers at very high premiums.
- Compared to the guideline companies, the subject company is smaller, has a lower historical and projected growth rate, and has key customer risk related to two large customers, which all support the selection of a lower multiples.

Income Approach Analyses

Questions to ask the valuation professional include:

- Of the two common income approach methods—the discounted cash flow (DCF) method and the capitalized single-period cash flow (CCF) method—which did you choose, and why?

- How does the subject company's projected performance compare to historical performance? And if projected performance is materially different from historical performance, why?
- How do the subject company's financial projections compare to prior-year projections?
- How does company management prepare projections? Does company management use a top-down approach (based on general industry growth) or a more granular, bottom-up approach (based on customer-by-customer or contract-by-contract projected growth)?
- Can the subject company achieve projected sales growth with its existing assets combined with the level of projected capital expenditures provided? Or will additional capital investments be necessary?
- How are the various components of the discount rate calculated?
- Was there any change in the discount rate inputs since the prior analysis (e.g., equity risk premium components, the company-specific risk premium, the cost of debt, or the debt-to-equity ratio)?
- How was the terminal value calculated, and if an exit multiple was used, what is the implied long-term growth rate?

Some examples of common and supportable responses include:

- The subject company is in a stable, mature industry with a stable projected growth rate, so the CCF method was used;
- The management-prepared projections are more conservative this year without any change in the company's underlying business, and the company has a history of exceeding its projections, so we used a lower company-specific risk premium this year; and
- The exit multiple used to calculate the terminal value implies a long-term growth rate of 5%, consistent with projected long-term industry and economic growth based on our research.

Identifying Common Mistakes

Another way a trustee can fulfill his or her obligation to remain engaged in the valuation process is by being aware of some of the most common mistakes made in valuations of ESOP-owned companies. While most valuation professionals strive to perform high-quality and supportable work, everyone occasionally make mistakes, and the trustee shouldn't be afraid to challenge the valuation firm if he or she comes across a flaw in the analysis. The following paragraphs outline several common mistakes made in valuations for which the trustee should be on the lookout.

Performing Only One Valuation Method

There are pros and cons to every valuation approach and method. For instance, market approach methods of analysis may be difficult to apply owing to a lack of publicly traded companies that are similar to the subject company in operations and size. Income approach methods are theoretically more sound but highly sensitive to several key assumptions that can be difficult to estimate. Therefore, a valuation professional should use a single method of analysis only if absolutely necessary, and should make every effort to perform a variety of different methods, which should be weighted accordingly based on relative strengths and weaknesses (to be documented in the report). (In some cases, however, using only one method may be unavoidable due to a complete lack of suitable guideline companies/transactions or credible financial projections.) Valuation professionals who use only one method lose the benefit of having alternative indications of value available to serve as a "reasonableness check."

Common Mistakes in the DCF Method

Mismatching Rates of Return with Cash Flow

Valuation professionals will sometimes blindly use a discount rate based on a weighted average cost of capital (WACC) without considering the level of projected cash flows being discounted. When performing a DCF method analysis, the valuation professional should ensure that the discount rate matches the level of cash flows. For instance, if the projected free cash flows are calculated after deductions for interest and principal payment on debt, the appropriate discount rate is the subject company's cost of equity—*not* the WACC—and the resulting indication of value will be the subject company's equity—*not* enterprise—value. If, on the other hand, the valuation professional is trying to estimate the subject company's enterprise value, then the projected cash flows should be calculated *before* deductions for interest and principal payments on debt, and the WACC should be used. Mismatching the discount rate with the level of cash flow can result in a material under- or over-valuation of the subject company, depending on whether the valuation professional seeks to estimate enterprise or equity value.

Improperly Tax-Affecting Cash Flows in the DCF Method

As anyone who works with ESOP companies knows, 100% ESOP-owned S corporations are exempt from federal income taxes. This is because S corporations pass corporate income through to shareholders for tax purposes, and ESOPs do not pay tax on this pass-through income. Therefore, a very common mistake made by valuation professionals without much ESOP company experience is to perform a valuation using the DCF method without deducting income tax expense from projected earnings. (A related but less egregious error is for the valuation professional to apply an S corporation premium to the valuation conclusion to reflect certain tax benefits enjoyed by pass-through entities, which may be appropriate for valuations performed for federal gift/estate tax purposes but not for ESOP purposes.) While this may seem to make sense at first blush, it is both inconsistent with the standard of "fair market value" by which ESOP company valuation professionals are bound and creates several practical issues for the company.

First, pursuant to Title I of ERISA and the proposed regulation relating to the definition of "adequate consideration" (Prop. Reg. Section 2510.3-18 (b)(2)(i)), "fair market value" is defined as the price at which an asset would change hands between a willing buyer and a willing seller, when the former is not under any compulsion to buy and the latter is not under any compulsion to sell, with both parties being willing and able to trade and being well-informed about the asset and the market for the asset. Implicit in this definition is the assumption of hypothetical buyers and sellers as opposed to any specific buyer or seller. The universe of potential buyers of ESOP-owned S corporations is largely comprised of tax-paying corporate entities, since the number of ESOP-owned S corporations relative to other types of companies is small. Therefore, a hypothetical willing buyer of an ESOP-owned S corporation would most likely be a tax-paying entity (i.e., either a C corporation subject to corporate taxes or a non-ESOP-owned S corporation subject to shareholder-level taxes), which would *not* pay a premium for the ESOP S corporation tax benefit since this benefit would not be transferable. Under the standard of "fair market value," therefore, the valuation professional should tax-affect the projected cash flows of an ESOP-owned S corporation as if it were a taxpaying entity.

Setting aside the theoretical error, failing to tax-affect projected earnings can also create a number of practical problems for the subject company. For instance, since excluding income tax expense from projected cash flows will likely result in a material overvaluation of the company, the company would effectively become unsellable, since no third-party buyer would be willing to match the ESOP price. (Another way to look at this would be to say that the discount for lack of marketability applicable to the valuation would offset any benefit derived from the tax-free cash flows.) In addition, the tax savings enjoyed by ESOP-owned S corporations is often needed to satisfy the ESOP repurchase obligation, so valuation professionals who exclude income tax expense from the DCF method without taking into consideration cash outflows related to the ESOP repurchase obligation are effectively "doubling down" on an inflated valuation.

Incorrectly Reflecting the Impact of an Acquisition

When valuing an ESOP company's equity, considering only the balance sheet impact of a recent acquisition may lead to an unsupportable decrease in value. This is because the full dilutive impact of the additional debt and/or cash reduction related to the acquisition is reflected on the company's balance sheet, but only a fraction of the revenue and earnings contribution of the acquired company may be reflected in the company's historical income statement. Therefore, in applying the market approach, the valuation professional should incorporate a pro-forma adjustment to reflect what the acquired company's full-year revenue and earnings contribution would have been. Alternatively, the valuation professional could simply disregard historical earnings metrics in the market approach and apply multiples to projected earnings and revenue metrics, which should incorporate the full-year impact of the acquired company. Finally, if the acquisition took place close to the valuation date, the valuation professional might even exclude the balance sheet impact of acquisition completely under the premise that the acquisition price paid is representative of fair market value and is therefore "value neutral" in the near term.

Improper Discounts for Lack of Control

Valuation professionals with limited ESOP company experience often value ESOP shares on a non-controlling interest basis, even when the ESOP itself owns a controlling interest, under the faulty premise that the shares in each participant's account represent a minority ownership interest of the company. While this may seem correct at first glance, the valuation professional's responsibility is to value the stock held by the ESOP trust *in total*, since the ESOP is technically a single shareholder of company stock (with ESOP shares beneficially allocated to individual participant accounts). Therefore, when deciding whether to apply a control premium or discount for lack of control, the valuation professional should perform his or her analysis on the ESOP's ownership stake and prerogatives of control in total rather than at the participant level.

Improper Discounts for Lack of Marketability

Valuation professionals with limited ESOP company experience may incorrectly apply a discount for lack of marketability in the 20% to 40% range, in line with the discounts applied in valuations of closely held stock for many other purposes. However, there is a significant difference between stock held by an ESOP and similar, closely held, non-ESOP stock in that there is a mandatory repurchase obligation (i.e., a "put" option) attached to the ESOP shares. This put option requires the ESOP company or trust to repurchase a participant's shares upon certain events, such as retirement, death, or disability. Therefore, the shares are marketable upon a distribution event.

The effect of the put option is that it greatly improves the marketability of the ESOP shares and the underlying liquidity of an ESOP participant's investment. Therefore, in the context of an ESOP company valuation, the existence of the put option will generally significantly reduce the discount for lack of marketability applicable to the ESOP shares, typically to the 5% to 10% range.

Not Addressing the ESOP Repurchase Obligation

As mentioned above, the ESOP put option represents the company's or ESOP trust's obligation to repurchase participant shares upon certain events. This put option creates a cash obligation for the company (either directly or indirectly), which is commonly known as the ESOP "repurchase obligation." The proper treatment of the repurchase obligation in the context of the valuation remains an evolving area within the ESOP company valuation community, and it can vary on a case-by-case basis.

In certain circumstances—such as if the ESOP ownership percentage is immaterial, if the company redeems and retires shares, or even if the corporate tax benefits associated with the ESOP far outweigh the projected repurchase obligation—the valuation professional may conclude that the repurchase obligation has no effect on the valuation.

In other instances—such as if the repurchase obligation prevents the company from making necessary investments to achieve growth—the valuation professional may account for the repurchase obligation implicitly, such as by selecting lower multiples or a higher discount for limited marketability. Some valuation professionals may account for the repurchase obligation of companies that engage in consistent share recycling explicitly by deducting the present value of the future repurchase obligation cost in excess of a normalized benefit amount.

While there may be many different ways to address the ESOP repurchase obligation, it must nonetheless be addressed. Therefore, if the valuation professional omits a discussion of the repurchase obligation from the valuation report, the trustee should ask the valuation professional how he or she considered this obligation in the valuation, and why he or she took this approach.

Adjustments for ESOP Contribution Expense

ESOP companies—especially those that have recently undergone a leveraged ESOP transaction—may often record a material "non-cash" ESOP contribution expense. This expense is "non-cash" in the sense that the ESOP will immediately use the contribution to pay principal and interest on the "inside" loan from the company, resulting in a net cash-neutral position for the company.

Since the ESOP contribution (as described here) represents a non-cash expense, the valuation professional will often add back the entire ESOP contribution expense to calculate the company's adjusted earnings. While this may be the correct procedure, it nonetheless requires some analysis. If, for instance, the ESOP company reduced or eliminated a preexisting benefit expense when the ESOP was installed—such as a 401(k) match or a profit sharing contribution—the valuation professional should deduct a normalized benefit expense to calculate adjusted earnings. This normalized benefit expense is often based on pre-ESOP benefit expense levels or market-based benefit expense metrics. If, on the other hand, the ESOP did *not* replace a preexisting benefit expense and represents a purely incremental, above-market benefit, then the valuation professional is correct to add back the entire ESOP contribution to calculate adjusted earnings.

Ignoring Excess Cash

Given the significant corporate tax benefits associated with ESOP ownership, ESOP-owned companies often build up material cash balances over time. Valuation professionals sometimes attribute little or no value to a subject company's cash balance under the premise that some level of cash is necessary to support working capital. However, in the context of private company acquisitions, it's common for an acquirer to "purchase" a target company's cash balance (as well as "excess" working capital above a certain specified target level) on a dollar-for-dollar basis as part of the overall acquisition price. Therefore, if the valuation professional attributes little or no value to cash, the valuation report should contain strong support as to why this cash is truly a component of working capital or is otherwise earmarked for some other liability or corporate obligation.

Conclusion

You don't have to be a valuation expert to remain engaged throughout the valuation process. By knowing the right questions to ask and being familiar with some of the most common mistakes in ESOP company valuations, internal trustees and corporate executives can ensure that their valuation firm is producing well thought-out, credible, and supportable analyses, which can go a long way in avoiding the practical issues that may arise from flawed valuations.

Chapter 3

What You Should Expect from Your ESOP TPA

Nancy Dittmer

Hilton Magic Corporation (HMC)[1] has maintained an ESOP since 2005. Originally, the ESOP owned 30% of HMC. That 30% ownership interest was acquired partially with a loan and partially with a purchase using cash that had accumulated in the ESOP before the purchase.

The 70% owner decided to sell another 21% of the stock to the ESOP on December 31, 2011, using the proceeds of a new loan. In 2012, the independent auditor for the ESOP discovered that the definition of compensation provided for in the plan document was not the same as what had been used in the operation of the plan. Due to the error discovered by the auditor and the complexity of a new loan, HMC decided to engage the services of a new ESOP third-party administrator (TPA).

The new TPA was engaged to provide the administration services for the year ended December 31, 2012. The information provided to the new TPA indicated that the ESOP had received dividends of $500,000 during 2012 and that all such dividends were applied to debt payments on the new loan. At that time, the TPA informed the CEO of HMC of the requirement that only the dividends paid with respect to the shares acquired with a particular loan can be applied to the repayment of that loan. The CEO was somewhat surprised because they had used the

---

1. This company is fictional, but the fact pattern is based on real-life situations encountered by ESOP companies.

dividends on the purchased shares to repay the first loan, and now he was being told that was not permissible.

The new TPA's services were expanded to include a review of the prior year's allocations followed by a voluntary correction filing with the Internal Revenue Service (IRS) and correction of the prior years' allocations for all of the errors discovered.

The new TPA welcomed the additional revenue, while the CEO of HMC vowed to learn exactly what he should be expecting from his TPA as well as his responsibilities with respect to the operation of the ESOP. The remainder of this chapter is intended to provide that information to ESOP sponsors.

It is important to define two terms before proceeding. The first term is *plan administrator* (PA). The PA is named in the plan document and is often the plan sponsor. The PA has a legal duty, as a named fiduciary, to act in the best interests of plan participants and exclusively for the purpose of providing benefits to the participants and their beneficiaries. The PA is therefore ultimately responsible for the operation of the ESOP, including:

- Collection and preparation of data used in the annual allocations
- Review and approval of annual allocation reports
- Filing of Form 5500 and distribution of summary annual reports
- Preparation of distribution forms and tax disclosures
- Selection and retention of plan advisors

The second term is *third-party administrator* (TPA). The TPA is an advisor hired by the PA to assist with the operation of the ESOP. The TPA is typically hired because of its knowledge of the requirements applicable to qualified retirement plans. The PA and TPA must work together on a collaborative basis because the TPA provides expertise but the fiduciary responsibility remains with the PA.

Before delving into what exactly you should expect from your ESOP TPA, I will first share a personal opinion. I believe it is very important to use the services of an ESOP TPA that has a group that specializes in ESOPs. While an ESOP and a 401(k) plan are both defined contribution qualified plans, there are significant differences in the administration of these plans. In a scenario like the one discussed above, the original TPA for the ESOP might not have worked with enough leveraged ESOPs to be aware of the dividend/debt repayment rule.

Now on to what services you should expect from your TPA. I have identified the following categories of related tasks, each of which is discussed in turn below:

- Census review/eligibility determination
- Trust reconciliation
- Participant level accounting and reporting
- Compliance testing
- Form 5500 preparation
- Distribution processing
- Legislative and regulatory updates

Census Review/Eligibility Determination

The TPA will ask the PA to provide the following information for each employee who received any compensation during the applicable plan year:

- Name
- Social Security number
- Date of birth
- Date of hire
- Date of termination, if any
- Reason for termination (e.g., identify death or disability)
- Date of rehire, if any
- Hours of service
- Compensation as defined in the plan document
- Officer status
- Ownership outside of the ESOP

- Any family relationships
- 401(k) deferrals
- Matching contribution if computed by the TPA for another plan
- Any other retirement plan contributions computed by the TPA for another plan

The TPA should review the provided census information to determine who is eligible for allocations of contributions and forfeitures in accordance with the terms of the plan document. Specifically, the TPA should identify employees who have satisfied the initial eligibility requirements and are now eligible to participate in the plan. The TPA should identify which participants have satisfied the accrual requirements for a current year contribution allocation (e.g., 1,000 hours of service and/or employment on the last day of the plan year). Also, any employees who are specifically excluded from participation in the plan according to the plan's terms should be identified.

The TPA should also identify the compensation to be used in the allocations. For example, for a new participant, compensation earned before his or her entry date may be excluded by the terms of the plan document.

One of the most common operational errors is when the definition of compensation provided to the TPA does not match the definition of compensation in the plan document. There are several alternative definitions, and it is important that both the TPA and the PA understand the specific definition used. If the compensation actually used in the allocations of employer contributions, forfeitures, and so on does not match the definition in the plan document, it is an operational error for failure to follow the terms of the plan document.

As a part of this process, it is typical for the TPA to review the census data for missing or inconsistent data. For example, the TPA may notice, based on Social Security numbers, that a new employee is actually a rehired employee even though no rehire date was provided. The TPA will typically review the information to make sure the compensation seems consistent with the hours worked, date of hire or termination, etc.

The end result should be a scrubbed employee census file showing the participants eligible for a current year allocation and the compensation to be used in such allocation. At this point, the TPA will likely send this eligibility determination back to the PA for review and final approval.

Trust Reconciliation

The TPA will request copies of the trust fund statements for the plan year. The TPA will also request information on accruals at the end of the year that are not reflected on the trust statements (e.g., accrued contributions). The TPA will prepare a balance sheet and income statement for review and approval by the PA. This balance sheet and income statement shall be the basis for the allocations to participants' accounts.

If the ESOP is leveraged, the TPA will use the information on the debt payments made for the plan year to calculate the shares to be released from the suspense account and allocated among participant accounts.

The IRS regulations provide that the general rule is that the shares released for any given year should be calculated as follows:

1. First, divide the principal and interest payments made for the current plan year by the principal and interest payments made, or to be made, for the current plan year and for all future years.
2. Then multiply the result in step 1 by the number of shares in the suspense account at the beginning of the plan year.

There is an alternative calculation that is based only on the principal payments made in the current year and scheduled to be made in future years, but that alternative is available only if the loan provides for level amortization over 10 years or fewer.

Participant-Level Accounting and Reporting

The next step is to perform the allocations to the participants' accounts, according to the specific terms of the ESOP document. This includes the following:

- Posting distributions/diversifications taken from participants' accounts
- Posting the forfeitures taken from terminated participants' accounts

- Recording and applying qualified domestic relations orders (QDRO)
- Allocating the employer contribution
- Allocating participant forfeitures
- Calculating and allocating shares released based on debt payments
- Allocating investment gains and losses, distinguishing between dividends on allocated shares or collateral
- Computing the vested status of participants
- Comparing a summary of accounts to the trust's assets
- Maintaining records of the participants' cost basis in their shares
- Preparing management reports of participant and total account balances for PA approval
- Preparing participant account statements for PA approval (the TPA may provide the participant statements to the PA for delivery to the participants or may mail the statements directly to the participants; the statements may also be provided electronically)

As noted above, the terms of the plan document will dictate the allocation methodologies. The TPA should also be aware of issues that are unique to ESOPs:

- ***Contributions:*** The most common method of allocating contributions among the accounts of ESOP participants is pro rata based upon compensation. If the contribution is a matching contribution, then its allocation will be according to the plan's specified matching formula.

  It may be possible to use another allocation formula, such as a combination of compensation and years of service. However, this would require that a nondiscrimination test be performed each year, and if the allocation does not satisfy the nondiscrimination requirements, then adjustments would need to be made. Most often those adjustments will limit the allocations to highly compensated employees.

  Other types of qualified plans are allowed to use an allocation formula that incorporates, to some degree, the Social Security contributions made by the employer. This is known as integration with Social Security or "permitted disparity." An ESOP is not allowed to use that allocation methodology.

Also, other qualified plans can perform any needed nondiscrimination testing that may apply to an alternative allocation formula on a "benefits" basis. This is known as cross-testing. An ESOP is not permitted to use cross-testing.

- **Source of forfeitures taken:** A partially vested participant's forfeiture must first be taken from the other investment accounts so that company stock is forfeited last. This can be problematic in that many of the systems used in qualified plan administration are set up to forfeit across all accounts on a pro-rata basis.

- **Dividends and S corporation distributions:** Any dividends or S corporation distributions on shares that are allocated in the participants' accounts will be allocated back to participant accounts based on those share balances.

  The allocation of the dividends or S corporation distributions on any shares that are in the unallocated suspense account can vary depending upon the ESOP. The ESOP document should specify how such amounts should be allocated. In many cases, those amounts are allocated in the same manner as an employer contribution (e.g., pro rata based on compensation). Some ESOP documents provide that the allocation of these amounts will be made in a manner similar to the allocated dividends or S corporation distributions (i.e., pro rata based on share account balances). There is a potential nondiscrimination issue here. While "earnings on balances in employees' accounts" will generally be allocated based on such account balances and not be subject to nondiscrimination testing, it is possible that the IRS would not consider the dividends or S corporation distributions on unallocated shares to be "earnings on balances in employees' accounts." This is one of those issues subject to different interpretations, so you should consult with your ESOP advisor.

- **Shares released based on debt payments made:** The method used to allocate the released shares back among the participants' accounts depends upon the source of the debt payments. So if an employer contribution was used to make the debt payment that year, then the allocation of the shares released will follow the same methodology used to allocate that contribution. If allocated dividends or S corporation distributions are used to make debt payments, then the shares released will be allocated back pro rata based on the share balances. The debt payments may be funded by more than one source, and if so, the allocation of the released shares will then be based on a combination of methodologies to match the source of the debt payments.

The use of dividends or S corporation distributions on allocated shares to make debt payments is subject to a value test. The value test is satisfied if the value of the shares allocated due to the debt payment made with the dividends/S corporation distributions is at least equal to the dollar amount of the dividend/S corporation distribution used. For example, if the dividend/S corporation distribution allocated to a participant's account is $100 and it is used to pay debt, then the participant's account will need to receive a share allocation with a value of at least $100 due to the debt payment made with that dividend/S corporation distribution. Satisfying the value test can be an issue simply due to a post-transaction drop in the value of the shares. It can also be more difficult if the value is decreasing due to company performance and/or general economic factors.

If the value test is not initially satisfied, it may be possible to correct by changing the allocation method of shares that are released from suspense due to the use of the dividends/S corporation distributions on unallocated shares to make debt payments. The allocation of the shares released due to the use of these unallocated dividends/S corporation distributions is often based on relative compensation rather than relative share balances. However, that allocation methodology can be modified to comply with the value test.

If there are not sufficient shares left in the suspense account to fully correct for the value deficiency, there are other possible corrections, including making an additional stock contribution, but there are potential obstacles to the use of these alternative corrections (e.g., an additional contribution may not be able to be made due to the limits on employer contributions). If you find yourself if this position, you will want to seek the advice of an experienced ESOP advisor.

- *Rebalancing:* Rebalancing is a method of ESOP participant accounting that is used by some ESOP sponsors. The ESOP plan document must include the rebalancing provisions for them to be applied. When an ESOP uses the rebalancing method of accounting, all allocations of contributions, forfeitures, share releases, earnings, etc. are made as normal. Then as a final step, all accounts of all participants are rebalanced so that all are in the same proportion of company stock and other investments. If the total ESOP assets are as follows:

    Company stock = $7,000,000
    Other investments = $3,000,000
    Total = $10,000,000

    Then after rebalancing, each participant's individual account will also be 70% company stock and 30% other investments.

- *Reshuffling:* Many ESOP sponsors choose to "segregate" or "convert" the accounts of former employees out of company stock and instead invest such accounts in more liquid and diversified investments. The ESOP document will outline the procedures for segregating the accounts of former employees out of company stock, including when the segregation should occur and ordering rules if there is not enough cash available to segregate all of the accounts of all former participants.

Also, there may be circumstances that necessitate that the company stock (and the related other investment or cash account) should be maintained in its own separate "bucket." The following is not intended to be an all-inclusive list but does include many of the more significant reasons for separate tracking:

- *Section 1042 shares:* Shares acquired in a tax-deferred sale to an ESOP under Section 1042 of the Internal Revenue Code (the "Code") are subject to certain restrictions against allocating such shares to the selling shareholder, certain family members and other more-than-25% shareholders. Thus, the Section 1042 shares should be tracked separately from any non-1042 shares. If there are multiple 1042 transactions, there may be a need for a separate bucket for each transaction.

- **Dividends:** Dividends and S corporation distributions may generally be applied only to the repayment of the loan incurred to acquire those shares. (However, there is a special exception for dividends on shares acquired on or before August 4, 1989.) So, if your ESOP has two loans outstanding, only the dividends or S corporation distributions paid on the shares acquired with loan no. 1 can be used to repay loan no. 1, and the same would be true for loan no. 2. Also, if your ESOP has shares that were not acquired with a loan, the dividends or S corporation distributions on such shares are not available to make payments on any loan. As a result, shares acquired in different leveraged transactions should be maintained in separate buckets.

- **Cost basis:** Shares acquired in different transactions will have a different cost basis. The most efficient method of tracking cost basis will likely be to maintain the shares acquired in different transactions in separate buckets.

- **Forfeitures:** In certain circumstances, forfeitures attributable to leveraged shares do not have to be included as annual additions for purposes of Code Section 415 testing. For your plan to exclude these forfeitures, the leveraged shares likely will need to be tracked separately from any purchased shares.

- **Diversifications:** Shares acquired after December 31, 1986, are subject to the Code's diversification provisions applying to those aged 55 with 10 years of service. Shares acquired before that date are not necessarily subject to these requirements, but they could be if your ESOP document so provides.

- **Distributions**
    - Shares that were acquired after December 31, 1986, are subject to the special distribution rules applicable to ESOPs. These rules govern the timing and form of distributions. Shares acquired on or before December 31, 1986, do not have to be subject to these rules unless the plan document so provides.
    - The ESOP document may delay distributions of share balances until the loan used to purchase such shares is completely repaid. In that situation, such shares should be tracked separately from other shares that may need to be distributed earlier.

- Any shares attributable to either safe harbor or money purchase pension plan contributions are subject to restrictions prohibiting in-service distributions and accordingly should be tracked separately from shares not subject to these restrictions.
- *Plan mergers:* If another plan's balances were merged into your ESOP at some point, those balances may have different benefits, rights, or features (such as the right to certain forms of payment, timing of distributions, in-service withdrawal options, etc.) attached to such balances that may need to be preserved.
- *Section 409(p) profit sharing transfers:* If an ESOP maintained by an S corporation is on the verge of failing the Code Section 409(p) testing, shares can be transferred into a profit-sharing component of the ESOP to avoid such failure. The S corporation income attributable to such shares will be subject to unrelated business income tax.

Compliance Testing

An ESOP, like any qualified retirement plan, is subject to a myriad of qualification requirements. In general, these requirements are designed to ensure that the ESOP provides for nondiscriminatory benefits within certain limits. The TPA should perform the following tests if they are applicable to your ESOP (section references are to the Code):

- *Section 410(b) minimum coverage test*: This test is designed to ensure that the group of employees participating in the ESOP is nondiscriminatory.
- *Section 401(a)(4) nondiscrimination compliance*: This test is designed to ensure that the allocations made among employee accounts do not discriminate in favor of highly compensated employees.
- *Section 414(b), (c), (m), (n), and (o) controlled group and leased employee requirements:* The above coverage and nondiscrimination tests must be performed considering all employees working for an organization within a controlled group.
- *Section 414(s) requirements*: If the ESOP document defines compensation to exclude certain items such as overtime or bonuses, there is a test to determine whether that definition is nondiscriminatory.

- *Section 415 annual additions limit:* The maximum annual allocation of contributions and forfeitures to a participant's account is the lesser of $51,000 or 100% of his or her compensation (as of 2013; this amount is indexed for inflation). All contributions and forfeitures to all defined contribution plans must be aggregated for this test. In certain situations, employer contributions applied to interest payments on a loan and forfeitures attributable to leveraged shares do not have to be counted for purposes of this limit.

- *Section 416 top-heavy test:* It must be determined whether your plan is "top-heavy." A plan is top-heavy if, as of the determination date, the total account value of key employees exceeds 60% of the total account value of all employees in the plan. This test is also an aggregate test that includes other retirement plans. When a plan is top-heavy or deemed top-heavy, certain minimum contributions are required.

- *Section 404 maximum deductible contribution:* The maximum annual contribution that can be deducted by the plan sponsor is generally 25% of the compensation of the employees participating in the plans. All employer contributions to all defined contribution plans must be aggregated for this test. Contributions in excess of the limit are not deductible by the plan sponsor and are subject to a 10% excise tax. There is a special deduction limit for a C corporation that allows contributions of 25% of compensation for principal payments. The contributions applied to interest payments are deductible regardless of the 25% limit. Further, the IRS has ruled that the 25% limit for principal payments is distinct from the general 25% contribution limit, so a C corporation could make two separate 25% contributions (assuming the contributions could be allocated without exceeding the Section 415 annual addition limits).

- *Section 401(a)(9) required distributions:* Any participants who have terminated employment and attained age 70½ must receive minimum distributions on an annual basis.

- *Section 409(n):* Code Section 409(n) provides that certain employees are prohibited from receiving an allocation of the shares acquired in a Section 1042 transaction, an allocation in lieu of such Section 1042 share allocations, and/or earnings on the Section 1042 shares.

The employees who are subject to these prohibitions (the "prohibited group") include the selling shareholder, an individual who is related to the selling shareholder (although there is an exception for limited allocations to lineal descendants) and any more-than-25% shareholder of the company.

- *Section 409(p):* In an effort to shut down "abusive" S corporation ESOPs that did not convey broad-based employee ownership, Congress promulgated the anti-abuse rules of Section 409(p). While these rules were aimed at abusive S corporation ESOPs, they apply to all S corporation ESOPs and do affect certain ESOPs that would normally not be considered abusive. The consequences of failing the Code Section 409(p) rules are draconian. The details of the anti-abuse rules are quite complex and are discussed in detail in other NCEO publications, such as the book *S Corporation ESOPs*.

Form 5500 Preparation

The TPA will typically prepare the Form 5500, including all schedules, based on the information accumulated in the prior steps. The summary annual report (SAR) will also be prepared by the TPA.

If the ESOP is subject to an independent audit, the TPA may accumulate and transmit the information requested by the auditor as well as address questions on such information.

Distribution Processing

The degree of involvement by the TPA in the processing of distribution and diversification payments will vary based on the arrangements made between the TPA and the PA.

It is fairly common for the TPA to provide a schedule that shows the terminated participants who are currently eligible for a distribution from the ESOP and the amount of the distribution. Similarly, the TPA often prepares a diversification schedule that identifies those participants eligible to diversify and the amount.

The PA may decide to have the TPA prepare the individual distribution/diversification election form packages. Alternatively, the PA may choose to prepare those forms based on the distribution/diversification schedules prepared by the TPA.

If the TPA is preparing the distribution/diversification forms, the PA may also want to have the forms returned directly to the TPA. The TPA can then prepare a directive for payment to the trustee to be approved by the PA.

In some instances, these distribution processing services can be provided electronically.

The TPA may also be hired to prepare the Forms 1099R, 1096, 945, and so on.

Legislative and Regulatory Updates

Often the PA will rely on the TPA to provide updates on legal and regulatory developments that could affect the operation of the ESOP.

Chapter 4

Best Practices for ESOP Trustees

James Staruck and Patrick DeCraene

We took over as successor trustee for an ESOP that had hired experienced ESOP legal counsel, an experienced third-party recordkeeper, an experienced valuation advisor, and even an institutional trustee. Unfortunately, although the advisors were all experienced, they did not communicate with each other very well.

The recordkeeper had not spoken with the prior trustee or legal counsel. The recordkeeper did not question the trust accounting statements when the trust statement reflected activity that was contrary to what the plan sponsor said had transpired. Legal counsel was not brought up to speed regularly, was involved only when the plan needed amending, and had no idea there were potential prohibited transactions. By examining the trust statements and the participant allocation reports, it appeared the prior trustee did not review the allocation summary or question the differences between the allocation reports and the trust accounting statements.

It takes a little effort to clear these issues up, but if they are left unattended and discovered upon government audit or investigation, they can mean disqualification of the plan and penalties for the fiduciaries. All it would have taken to keep things under control is a conversation between the parties to discuss the discrepancies between what the plan sponsor communicated and what the recordkeeper and trustee each understood was being communicated. Once these discrepancies were vetted, legal counsel could have come up with a solution to reconcile the records and prevent the misunderstanding from recurring in the future.

While each of the parties needed to step up at some point, two of the parties involved, the plan sponsor and the trustee, had all of the information to know there were potential problems, and both of them had fiduciary duties to keep in mind. Of these two, the trustee is expected to be more knowledgeable and should have been the one to investigate immediately.

Too often, the trustee is seen only as the party that sets the value of the company stock every year or the party that approves the purchase or sale of stock. The trustee's duties go much deeper. In addition to valuing the shares, the trustee is the one who will cast the vote, on behalf of the shares owned by the ESOP, for the board of directors. The trustee is charged with providing a full and correct accounting of the trust activity to the appropriate parties, as outlined in the trust agreement. Very often the trustee will take custody of trust assets or at least hire an appropriate custodian. None of these duties can be viewed in isolation.

The fiduciary duties of an ESOP trustee are the same regardless of whether the trustee is an independent, corporate trustee or whether the trustee is an insider, such as the chief financial officer or vice president of human resources. This chapter describes the duties of an ESOP trustee, the best practices for carrying out those duties, and what can go wrong when a trustee fails to carry out those duties.

What Does a Trustee Do and What Are Best Practices?

Following ERISA Duties

The Employee Retirement Income Security Act of 1974 (ERISA) provides a very clear definition of the five primary duties of fiduciaries to qualified retirement plans: (1) act solely in the interest of plan participants and their beneficiaries; (2) carry out their duties with the same diligence as a prudent man acting in a similar capacity under similar circumstances; (3) follow plan documents unless the documents are inconsistent with ERISA; (4) diversify plan investments; and (5) pay only reasonable plan expenses. ESOPs, properly designed and administered, are exempt from the duty of diversification. Therefore, the duty to diversify plan investments does not apply to a trustee. However, the other four duties do apply.

Following Plan and Trust Documents

A trustee must follow the terms of the plan and trust documents. To do so, the trustee must ensure that it has complete and accurate copies of each document, including all relevant amendments thereto. The trustee must have a thorough understanding of each document. Legal counsel can be very helpful in educating the trustee as to the operation of certain plan and trust document provisions.

While a trustee should familiarize itself with all the plan and trust document provisions, we would like to point out two provisions that a trustee should be especially cognizant of: voting shares in the ESOP and investing cash within the ESOP. The trustee should determine whether it is *directed or discretionary* as to these items. Being directed means that the trustee will receive a direction from certain identified individuals within the company as to how to vote the shares (or which director nominees to vote in favor of) and/or investing the cash. Being discretionary means that the trustee can exercise its sole discretion and judgment with respect to these matters.

If the trustee is directed, it is arguable that the trustee's liability under law is limited as to the determination of the propriety of the direction received. If the trustee is discretionary, then the trustee's liability with respect to these matters may be greater. Plan sponsors should determine how much liability they want to keep for themselves when determining whether the trustee should be directed or discretionary.

When it comes to purchases or sales of qualifying employer securities, the trustee generally acts in a discretionary capacity. Occasionally, the trust agreement may indicate that the trustee is directed in these areas. If so, it is important to be sure that the trust agreement goes on to say that the trustee has the responsibility to override the direction if following the direction would cause the trustee to breach its fiduciary duty. Note that the difference between a directed trustee's duties and a discretionary trustee's duties in purchases and sales is very small. In both cases, the trustee must be very aware of its duty of prudence.

We always see trustees acting in a directed capacity for participant distributions. Institutional trustees do not have the knowledge of the employment status of the participants. Therefore, the plan sponsor must give the direction. Internal trustees should be looking for direction in these cases as well as for separation-of-duty purposes.

Valuing Stock

One of the most visible and important responsibilities an ESOP trustee undertakes is setting the value of the employer securities. The value must be set at least annually, but may be more frequently if the ESOP plan document so provides. It is worth noting that the ESOP trustee, not the trustee's valuation advisor, determines the value. The trustee's financial advisor *recommends* the value to the trustee. However, it is ultimately the trustee's decision as to what the value should be, and it will be the trustee that is held liable for a faulty value.

Determining the value of employer stock is the single most litigious issue in the ESOP world. Whether the value is being set for a purchase or sale transaction or simply a quarterly, semi-annual, or annual update to the value, a trustee must follow a prudent process.

The process begins with the selection of an independent, qualified valuation firm. The trustee should be comfortable that its financial advisor possesses the qualifications and skill necessary to perform an ESOP valuation. We recommend that a trustee perform some due diligence about its financial advisor's qualifications to perform ESOP valuations before selecting the advisor. For example, the trustee should ask the prospective financial advisor how many ESOP valuations the advisor has performed in the past. We also recommend that the trustee review sample ESOP valuation reports from the prospective financial advisor before engaging the advisor. If the trustee is an independent trustee and works with many different financial advisors, we recommend that the trustee maintain a list of approved financial advisors and a set of procedures required in order for a financial advisor to be put on, and removed from, the list.

In addition, the trustee's financial advisor should be *independent*. This generally means that the financial advisor should not also be performing work for the company or any of its affiliates. In a transaction, the trustee's financial advisor should not have performed work for the seller, the company, or any of their representatives. The point is that the parties to the transaction should be truly independent to ensure the transaction is negotiated at arms' length.

Once the financial advisor is selected, the next step is to conduct a thorough due diligence review with management. It is a best practice for the trustee to attend the due diligence review of the company with the trustee's financial advisor rather than merely send the financial advisor to attend without the trustee. A thorough due diligence review includes a review and discussion of the year-end financial statements, the projected financial statements, the overall industry, the competitors, the suppliers, the customers, key personnel changes, management succession, new product or service offerings, the backlog, the pipeline, litigation, and any other relevant items. One of the questions we often ask executives at our ESOP companies when conducting due diligence is "What keeps you up at night?" We are often surprised at the information we receive when executives answer this question honestly.

Both the quantitative aspects (the numbers) and the qualitative aspects (the story behind the numbers) are very important for the trustee to understand. For example, with regard to projections, if the growth rates in the projected cash flows are significantly different than the historical growth rates in the cash flows, the trustee should understand why, i.e., what has changed with regard to the company's business, the industry, or the economy in general that would cause the deviation, and what the bridge is between the historic numbers and the projected numbers.

Following due diligence, the trustee's financial advisor will compile a full valuation report and deliver it to the trustee for further review. We recommend that the financial advisor provide the report to the trustee at least a day or two in advance of the trustee's meeting with the financial advisor to determine the share price. That way, the trustee has time to review the report. This is important because the trustee is charged with understanding the report, not simply accepting it. All methodological assumptions need to be understood.

The trustee should also be alert to any changes in methodologies within the valuation. One way to do this is to create a checklist that lines up the methodologies and variables within those methodologies year-over-year. For example, if the trustee's financial advisor has historically used the discounted cash flow method and guideline company method to value the stock and weighted those methods equally but is now placing 75% of the weight on the discounted cash flow method, the trustee should understand why. The checklist we recommend is a way to flag these changes so that the trustee can inquire of its financial advisor as to the reasons why.

The trustee should also ensure that repurchase obligation is considered as part of the valuation. The trustee and its financial advisor should question the company to determine that a repurchase analysis, whether conducted internally or by an independent third party, has been completed. If there is a significant opportunity cost associated with the company's obligation to repurchase shares, then the trustee may want to consider whether there is some impact to the share value. For example, it may be that the company's repurchase obligation is so large that it is hindering the company's future growth plans. In this case, the trustee may feel that the share value should be affected to some degree by the repurchase obligation. On the other hand, if the company is generating sufficient cash flow to meet its repurchase obligation and fund growth, then the trustee may believe that no effect on the value is warranted. The bottom line is that the trustee should be aware of the repurchase obligation and how it may affect the company's operations.

Voting Stock

Another important trustee duty is voting the shares in the election of the board of directors or some other corporate action. This responsibility is not ignored in the Department of Labor (DOL) regulations. In fact, the duty to act solely in the interest of the plan participants speaks directly to this issue. A trustee, internal or external, must make a fully independent decision in these cases. Proper documentation of the process followed in reaching that decision is paramount. Often, the trustee acts in a directed capacity while voting. Even when directed, the trustee has a duty to be sure that the direction is proper and that following the direction does not violate the trustee's duty of prudence.

The frequency with which the trustee votes the shares is determined by the company's bylaws. Thus, a trustee should obtain a copy of the company's bylaws and become familiar with the voting provisions contained therein. For instance, the trustee should be aware what the minimum and maximum number of directors is, how the nominating process works, who replaces a director who has resigned or been removed, how long director terms are, etc.

In instances where a "pass-through" vote is required, which are outlined in the Internal Revenue Code, the trustee must ensure that participants have received all information material to the decision they are being asked to make, that participants have been given enough time to review the materials and ask questions (we recommend not less than 21 days, if practicable) and that their directions will be kept confidential. It is worth noting that in these "pass-through" cases, the participants are not voting their shares; rather, they are directing the trustee as to how they want their allocated shares voted. Thus, it is incumbent upon the trustee to go through a process designed to determine the prudence of following participant directions. The trustee must also look to the ESOP plan document to determine how to vote unallocated shares and how to vote allocated shares for which no participant directions have been received.

Occasionally, a trustee will be asked to consent to or approve matters that are normally within the purview of the board. This most often occurs when the board does not have "disinterested" or independent directors. For instance, if the board is comprised only of members of the executive management team and they are looking to approve a stock appreciation rights plan of which they will be the beneficiaries, they may ask the trustee to consent as a means of protecting their decision. If the board had "disinterested" directors who could approve this decision, then this decision would be solely within the purview of the board and not one for the trustee. In this case, the trustee would have to go through a prudent process, which may involve its financial advisor, legal counsel, and even an outside compensation consultant, in order to give a prudent approval.

Trust Administration/Accounting

While not necessarily a fiduciary action, the production of annual trust accounting statements is a duty of the trustee. Often, an individual trustee will engage a custodian to hold the plan assets and issue the statements. Trustees also engage providers for other administrative responsibilities that are assigned to the trustee in the trust agreement. This allocation of administration responsibilities is proper and encouraged. The duty to act with prudence suggests strongly that a trustee who is not experienced in a given matter must rely on advice from someone who does have that experience. Thus, trustees can act prudently by surrounding themselves with knowledgeable people, provided the trustees conduct proper due diligence in the selection process.

Monitoring the Board of Directors

Typically, an independent trustee does not serve on the company's board of directors. Nor does the trustee function as a board member. That being said, the trustee does have a duty to monitor the board. Monitoring the board typically extends to major board decisions and corporate actions like the acquisition of a target company, the disposition or sale of a major corporate division, the issuance of a significant amount of debt, etc.

It is important to note that these types of actions typically do not require the affirmative vote or consent of the shareholders of the company, like the ESOP trust. However, because these types of major corporate actions could affect the value of the stock held in the ESOP, the trustee should take steps to understand the magnitude of these decisions on the ESOP.

For example, if the board and executive management team desire that the company acquire a target for a purchase price that is material, this decision would not require shareholder/trustee approval under corporate law. However, it would invoke the trustee's duty to monitor. The trustee can fulfill its duty by gaining a thorough understanding of the board's rationale for the decision (e.g., why does the acquisition make sense for the shareholders?), the board's process in coming to the decision (e.g., what other companies did the board consider acquiring?, how was the purchase price derived?, why does the purchase price make sense?), and what the effect on the ESOP will be. It may be that the trustee must enlist the services of its financial advisor to determine the economic impact to the ESOP.

Monitoring can also be accomplished by periodically attending board meetings. Most corporate trustees find it necessary to remain independent from the board; thus, an invitation to attend board meetings is probably appropriate. The board should feel comfortable in allowing the shareholders to obtain firsthand experience in their meeting process. Therefore, it is important for trustees to remain professional and honor the procedures within which they are invited to attend.

Overseeing Other Trust Assets

It is important to remember that a trustee is ultimately responsible for all trust assets, not just the stock held in the trust (unless, of course, the trustee's engagement agreement and the trust agreement specifically exclude these other assets from the responsibility of the trustee). Therefore, to the extent that there are other assets, like cash held in bank accounts or an investment account consisting of marketable securities, a best practice would dictate that those accounts be titled in the trustee's name and that the trustee have signing authority over the accounts. In addition, with respect to marketable securities, if the trustee has discretionary authority over these investments, the trustee should either manage those investments itself or hire an independent, qualified, investment advisor to manage the investments. If the trustee elects to hire a third party investment advisor to manage the marketable securities, the trustee then has a duty to monitor the performance of the selected investment advisor. This means that the trustee should frequently meet with its investment advisor to determine the suitability of the investments. The trustee should also ensure that the investment advisor's performance in managing the investments is adequate. If, for example, the returns on the investments ranked very low relative to comparable investments, then the trustee would need to either request that the investment advisor modify its investment approach or even select a new investment advisor. Further, the trustee should be aware of the fees being charged by the investment advisor and whether those fees are reasonable. In short, it is not enough for a trustee to hire a qualified investment advisor to manage non-employer securities and then walk away.

Further, a best practice would be for the trustee to obtain an investment policy statement from the company. The investment policy statement would discuss the risk profile of the plan and the returns expected as well as indicate the types of investments the company feels are suitable for the ESOP.

Negotiating Transactions

The trustee will be the party responsible for negotiating purchases and sales of stock by the ESOP. In these cases, the trustee will enlist its financial advisor to assist in reviewing the transactions and negotiations. A due diligence review of the type discussed above is crucial. In a transaction, the trustee will also need to review, and understand, all relevant transaction documents. The trustee's legal counsel can provide assistance in this regard. The trustee should be careful to negotiate the price, not merely accept the offer on the table.

Many transactions are financed in part by the sellers. In these cases, sellers often receive some form of subordinated promissory note with a warrant or other equity kicker attached. The trustee needs to evaluate the seller's combined rate of return for both the note and warrant and compare that rate to a market rate for similarly situated financiers. It is incumbent upon the trustee to understand the economics behind warrant and synthetic equity valuation in determining what the acceptable level of dilution should be.

As with all fiduciary decisions, it is important that the trustee properly document all of its negotiations and deliberations.

Engagement Agreements and Pricing

The relationship between an independent, corporate, or individual trustee and the company is contractual. The terms of the relationship should be set forth in an engagement agreement between the company and the trustee. The engagement agreement should specifically lay out what the trustee is being hired to do (e.g., serve as trustee for a transaction only, serve as ongoing trustee, etc.). This agreement will also set forth the fees the trustee will receive as consideration for its services. It is worth noting the circularity that arises because trustees are typically hired and removed by the company's board of directors, yet the trustee, in its capacity as shareholder, votes for the appointment of directors. This somewhat circular logic makes it especially important for an internal trustee to have some type of engagement agreement as well to clarify its fiduciary versus corporate responsibilities.

The trustee's fee is mutually agreed upon by the company and the trustee. The trustee's fee is usually a function of two variables: (1) the amount of work involved in serving as trustee and (2) the risk in serving as trustee. The risk is usually the risk of being named as a defendant in a lawsuit by either a private plaintiff or the DOL. Lawsuits usually arise after the company's stock has fallen significantly, thereby diminishing the value of the participants' retirement accounts.

It is often difficult to gauge the likelihood of a decline in stock value and thus the risk to the trustee. However, in accepting an engagement, a trustee should have a basic understanding of the company's business model and the volatility of the company's industry. Some of the questions a trustee may want to answer before accepting an engagement are: Does the trustee understand how the company makes money? Does the trustee have a basic understanding of the industry within which the company operates? What drives the company's profitability? How deep is the management team? Are there reasonably foreseeable events that could occur that would lead to a decline in cash flows? For example, if a company earns the majority of its revenue by providing services to the State of Illinois (which has the lowest credit rating of any of the 50 states), it may be reasonable for the trustee to assume that this company's business model is inherently more risky than it was years ago. Thus, the trustee should ensure that it is charging a fee that is commensurate with the risk of holding employer securities whose value is tied to the performance of the company.

A best practice would be for the trustee to review financial statements and interview management before accepting an engagement. In addition, the trustee may want to consider structuring its fee in a manner different than basing it upon the market value of the stock. If the fee is based upon the market value of the stock, then as the stock declines in value, so does the trustee's fee. Yet, as the market value of the stock declines, the trustee's risk actually increases.

What Can Go Wrong

As discussed above, the main area of trustee liability results from a drop in the stock value, which causes the participants' retirement accounts to decrease in value. Trustees need to be particularly careful when purchasing stock or selling stock. Where the trustee purchases stock, the trustee's exposure is to claims made by third parties (either a class of participants or the DOL) that the trustee paid more than adequate consideration for the stock, thereby resulting in a prohibited transaction. This risk becomes especially acute when the company fails to meet the projections that were used to develop the purchase price. This is not to say that a failure to meet projections is evidence of a prohibited transaction. However, it is something that the plaintiffs will use in bolstering their claims of a prohibited transaction.

Where the trustee sells stock, the trustee is exposed to claims that the ESOP sold the stock for less than *adequate consideration*. Trustees should take extra caution when selling shares back to the management team. In these cases, we recommend the negotiation of a "clawback" provision allowing the ESOP to regain additional proceeds if the stock is "flipped" by the buyers within a certain time frame.

A board of directors consisting solely of insiders is also an area of concern for a trustee. Best practices dictate that an ESOP company has at least one or two outside, independent board members. The implementation of outside board members removes conflicts of interest that may otherwise exist. This adds a level of protection to the decisions made by the board and protects the trustee in monitoring the board. In addition, outside board members add a different perspective and bring different experiences to bear that are often helpful in the boardroom.

Most ESOP plan sponsors go through some type of feasibility study before proceeding with a transaction. While many such studies concentrate on the price at which the stock will be transacted and some of the other deal terms, including synthetic equity and expected lending arrangements, the studies should also look closely at the ability of the plan sponsor to fund the debt service. Potential plan sponsors need to examine the funding level needed to pay down the inside note. If they expect to use contributions, the plan sponsor will need to make sure it has enough payroll to fund contributions under the Internal Revenue Code Section 415 limits. Very often a plan sponsor expects to fund some of the debt service with dividends or S corporation distributions. Section 415 does not apply in these cases, but there is another hurdle to overcome. Known as the "market value test" or the "dividend make whole rule," this hurdle presents a challenge when the debt is prepaid, which accelerates the allocation of shares at a time when the value of the shares falls well below the cost basis. The rule states that for a dividend to be deductible, the dividends paid on allocated shares and used to pay debt must be replaced with shares released by such payment in the same value as the dividend given up. For example, if $100 in dividends on allocated shares is used to pay the ESOP note, the holders of those allocated shares on which the dividend was paid need to be allocated $100 worth of shares. If the share value falls too far below the original cost basis and a large number of the shares are allocated, the loan payment may not release enough shares to "make the dividend whole." While there are remedies for this situation, they can be very expensive. It is wise for a trustee to examine the debt service funding before the transaction is complete.

These are just a few items a trustee needs to be aware of when making fiduciary decisions. Surrounding oneself with qualified, experienced advisors is the best way to ensure all the questions are asked and answered. However, as we discussed at the beginning of this chapter, even with experienced advisors, communicating is essential.

About the Authors

Patrick DeCraene is a vice president at GreatBanc Trust Company, which he joined in 2001. He has extensive experience in designing and administering qualified and nonqualified retirement plans, including defined benefit, 401(k), profit sharing, and 403(b) plans. Mr. De Craene received a BS in mathematics from Illinois Benedictine College. He is a CFP practitioner. Mr. DeCraene serves plan sponsors and their companies in designing and structuring their retirement plan needs.

Joe Demetrius, CFA, is an associate in the Washington, DC, office of Stout Risius Ross, Inc. His concentration is in ESOP and ERISA advisory services. He has experience in valuing business ownership interests in ESOPs, and has performed analyses related to ESOP security formation and transactions, determining transaction fairness and adequate consideration, and annual employer security valuation updates.

Nancy Dittmer is a senior vice president for Verisight, Inc. As the leader of the firm's ESOP administration and consulting practice, Nancy is responsible for all of its ESOP services. These include feasibility studies, repurchase obligation studies, annual participant accounting and reporting, etc. In addition to being a member of the board of directors of the NCEO, she authors the column "ESOP Operational Issues" for its Web site. She is a member of the ESOP Association (TEA) and is a past chair of TEA's administration advisory committee. She has also served on TEA's interdisciplinary advisory committee on fiduciary issues. Nancy is a member of the Employee-Owned S Corporations of America (ESCA).

Aziz El-Tahch, CFA, is a managing director in the New York City office of Stout Risius Ross, Inc. He has experience in valuing securities, intangible assets, and business interests for many purposes, including fairness and solvency opinions, mergers and acquisitions, corporate strategic planning, stock options and warrants, purchase price allocation, goodwill impairment testing, estate and gift taxation, shareholder disputes, and liability and damages analysis. He has extensive experience in valuing business ownership interests in ESOPs and has performed analyses related to ESOP security formation and transactions, determining transaction fairness and adequate consideration, and annual employer security valuation updates. Mr. El-Tahch graduated magna cum laude, Phi Beta Kappa from Georgetown University's Edmund A. Walsh School of Foreign Service with a concentration in economics. Aziz is a member of the CFA Institute, the New York Society of Security Analysts, the Association for Corporate Growth, the National Center for Employee Ownership, and the ESOP Association, where he serves as an officer on the executive committee of the New York/New Jersey chapter.

Kevin Long is a shareholder in the law firm of Chang Ruthenberg & Long PC. His practice focuses on all facets of ESOPs, including corporate succession planning, mature ESOPs, fiduciary representation, and DOL/IRS defense, and all aspects of related nonqualified and equity deferred compensation planning for ESOP companies. Over the last 25 years, he has advised over 250 ESOPs and ESOP companies, ranging from professional firms to manufacturers. Kevin is a California State Bar Certified Specialist in Taxation. He authored the ESOP-A and Certified Pension Consultant (CPC) course materials on ESOPs for the American Society of Pension Professionals and Actuaries (ASPPA), and he teaches coursework on ESOPs for the California CPA Educational Foundation. He is a fellow of the American College of Employee Benefits Counsel and is listed in Best Lawyers in America.

Corey Rosen is the founder and former executive director of the National Center for Employee Ownership (NCEO) and now is its senior staff member. He cofounded the NCEO in 1981 after working for five years as a professional staff member in the U.S. Senate, where he helped draft legislation on employee ownership plans. Before that, he taught political science at Ripon College. He is the author or coauthor of over 100 articles and many books on employee ownership, and a coauthor (with John Case and Martin Staubus) of *Equity: Why Employee Ownership Is Good for Business* (Harvard Business School Press, 2005). He has lectured on employee ownership on six continents, has appeared frequently on CNN, PBS, NPR, MSNBC, and other network programs, and is regularly quoted in the *Wall Street Journal,* the *New York Times, BusinessWeek,* and other leading publications. He holds a Ph.D. in political science from Cornell University.

James Staruck is the president and CEO of GreatBanc Trust Company, where he specializes in ESOP transactions and special fiduciary assignments. Mr. Staruck's ESOP responsibilities have included negotiating structuring purchases and sales of public and privately held companies by ESOPs, and his special fiduciary responsibilities have included negotiating and approving settlements on behalf of qualified retirement plans involved in stock drop litigation under ERISA and related claims under federal securities laws. Mr. Staruck also serves as a member on the ESOP Association's Legislative and Regulatory Committee. Mr. Staruck received a JD from the DePaul University College of Law; an MBA, with an emphasis in finance, from DePaul University's Kellstadt Graduate School of Business; and a BS in finance from the University of Illinois, Champaign-Urbana. He is a member of the Chicago Bar Association.

About the NCEO

The National Center for Employee Ownership (NCEO) is widely considered to be the leading authority on employee ownership in the U.S. and the world. Established in 1981 as a nonprofit information and membership organization, it now has over 2,500 members, including companies, professionals, unions, government officials, academics, and interested individuals. It is funded entirely through the work it does.

Our mission is to provide the most objective, reliable information possible about employee ownership at the most affordable price possible. As part of the NCEO's commitment to providing objective information, it does not lobby or provide ongoing consulting services. The NCEO publishes a variety of materials on employee ownership and participation, holds dozens of seminars, conference calls, Webinars, and conferences on employee ownership annually, and offers a variety of online courses. To join the NCEO, go to www.nceo.org/join or call us at 510-208-1300. An introductory NCEO membership costs $90 for one year ($100 outside the U.S.) and covers an entire company at all locations, a single professional offering services in this field, or a single individual with a business interest in employee ownership. Members receive :

- Our main newsletter *Employee Ownership Report,* plus a PDF newsletter on equity compensation;
- Discounts on our many publications, events, and other resources;
- Dozens of free live Webinars on ESOPs and equity compensation every year;
- Access to the members-only area of our Web site, including a database of service providers, archives of newsletters and other resources, a discussion forum, and more; and
- The right to call or email with questions.

Order Form

This book is published by the National Center for Employee Ownership (NCEO) and costs $10 each for NCEO members and $15 each for nonmembers, in print or digital format (see below for tax and shipping information). To order, go to our Web site at www.nceo.org; telephone us at 510-208-1300; fax this order form to 510-272-9510; or send this order form to NCEO, 1736 Franklin Street, 8th Floor, Oakland, CA 94612. If you join as an NCEO member with this order or are already an NCEO member, you will pay the discounted member price. See www.nceo.org for dozens of other publications on employee ownership.

Name

Organization

Address

City, State, Zip (Country)

Telephone   Fax   Email

Method of Payment: ☐ Check (payable to "NCEO")   ☐ Visa   ☐ M/C   ☐ AMEX

Credit Card Number

Signature   Exp. Date

Checks are accepted only for orders from the U.S. and must be in U.S. currency.

Title *(specify print or digital version)*	Qty.	Price	Total

Tax: California residents add 9% sales tax (on print publications only, not membership or digital publications)	Subtotal	$
	Sales Tax	$
Shipping: In the U.S., first print publication $5, each add'l $1; elsewhere, we charge exact shipping costs to your credit card, plus a $10 handling surcharge; no shipping charges for membership or digital publications	Shipping	$
	Membership	$
Introductory NCEO Membership: $90 for one year ($100 outside the U.S.)	TOTAL DUE	$